Generis
PUBLISHING

I0834023

The Role of Religious Leader in Maintaining Peace

Adeloye Gabriel Oludele

Title: *The Role of Religious Leader in Maintaining Peace*

Author: *Adeloye Gabriel Oludele*

ISBN: 978-1-63902-563-3

Cover image: www.pixabay.com

Publisher: Generis Publishing
Online orders: www.generis-publishing.com
Contact email: info@generis-publishing.com

TABLE OF CONTENTS

Introduction

Religion is said to be one of the significant phenomena in human experience. It is a major force in enhancing the development of a society as well as retarding its growth (Otonko, 2012, 352). Religious groups in Nigeria have helped in one way or the other to better the lots of the inhabitants of the land especially through its social responsibilities. While at the same times lack of understanding and cooperation among some religious adherents have adversely affected the country. Religion must help us to truly recognize our common humanity by listening to one another instead of talking to one another (Akinwale 2012: 236) but what is happening in Nigeria today in the name of religion is disgust and discord There are many horrible reports of crises, killing people and destruction of properties all in the name of defending and proclaiming a religious faith. The menace today is not only between Christian and Muslim worshippers as so many people think but it exists among the three major religions recognize by the government of Nigeria. The submission of Rotimi Omotoye buttresses this claim that most religious crises in Yorubaland, Nigeria were among the practitioners of the three major religions (Omotoye 2012: 335). He mentioned for instance, the religious misunderstanding between the Muslims and the worshippers of Moremi goddess in Offa, Kwara state. The Muslims in Offa according to him made several attempts to demolish Moremi shrine in the present location because of its closeness to the Offa Central Mosque. The matter was however lay to rest when the eminent Yoruba leaders including the paramount ruler of Offa land advocated for the retention of the shrine as a mark of honour to Moremi because of her role in defending the Ile-Ife people against the invasion of the Igbo (Omotoye, 2012, 335).

Similarly according to Omotoye some members of *Egungun* (Masquerade) cults went into an Anglican church in Omuaran, Kwara state to embarrass the members of the church. The police later arrested the said *Egungun* cults. (Omotoye 2012: 336). Christians as well through their song usually ridicule the *Egungun* (Masquerade) worshippers that the one call masquerade is an ordinary human being like them therefore the Christians should not be afraid of them. One can therefore accept the submission of Osaghae and Suberu that masquerade religious activities have been a major source of conflicts in some parts of Nigeria (Osaghae & Suberu 2005: 11)

This writing thus becomes very important because of the present situation of the country where terrorism, banditry, ritual killings, Boko haram insurgence, menace of the Fulani herdsmen and kidnapping are prevailing. Since religion is not only a spiritual affair but the entire existence of man (such as emotional, physical, mental, psychological and ethical). Religion therefore, has major role to play in maintaining peace and order in a society and the religious leaders must be a leading example in promoting peace. The expectation of the writer of this work is that the adherents of various religious groups would embrace peace and allow religious adherents to practice their faith without disturbance. It is also hope that the Government would not favour one faith above others but allow religious freedom because Nigeria is a secular state with a constitution that guarantees freedom of thought, conscience and religion. The Nigerian Constitution clearly indicates that "the Government of the federation or state shall not adopt any religion as a State religion". So as the Constitution makes provision for the citizens' freedom of thought, conscience and religion, the Government should thereby create good atmosphere for citizens to practice their chosen religion.

CHAPTER ONE

THE RELIGIOUS GROUPS IN NIGERIA

Nigeria as a Nation

It is appropriate to start with a brief introduction of the Nation called Nigeria before describing the religions in the country. According to Abogunrin, the gradual process of the creation of the nation – Nigeria by the British colonial authority began in 1861 when the Lagos's colony was captured. Oil protectorate was then established in 1885 and redesignated in 1893 as the Niger coast protectorate. The northern and southern protectorate was established between 1900 and 1906 and the amalgamation of the southern Nigeria protectorate with the northern Nigeria protectorate by the Governor – General, Lord Fredrick Lugard into one nation was in 1914 (Abogunrin, 2001, 2 & 3). The northern and the southern protectorate thus formed the name Nigeria.

Nigeria is a country in West Africa bordering Niger in the north, Chad in the northeast, Cameroun in the east and Benin in the west. This nation is a federal Republic comprising presently thirty six states and Abuja as the federal capital territory. Nigeria became independent on October 1st 1960 and has been experiencing incessant crises since then starting with the civil war from1967 to 1970. Nigeria is divided roughly in half between Muslims who live mostly in the north and Christians, who live mostly in the south (Wikipedia, March, 2021).

Nigeria has a population of over 200 million with three major religious groups, African Traditional religion, Christianity and Islam. The African Traditional religion is the indigenous religion of the people, Islam and Christianity came into the country to competite with the traditional religions. To be precise, Islam came to Nigeria through the northeast in the eleventh century and spread in the early 1800s during the Jihad of Usman Dan Fodio (Umejesi, 1992, 85 – 92), while Christianity gained access through Badagry in 1842 (Ajayi, 1965, 31). Though, there had been attempt to Christianize the present Nigeria in the 15th century through the missionary efforts of the Augustinian and Capuchin monks from Portugal who came to introduce Christian faith in Benin and Warri Kingdoms. It however failed because of the missionaries were more interested in commerce than gospel (Ayandele, 1966, 6). J. F. Ade Ajayi however blamed *Oba* (the King) of Benin for the failure. According to him, the King dismissed the Portuguese missionaries and suggested that they could return when he had much time that he could spare on leisure. When they eventually returned in 1538, the king was no more interested in the religion (Ajayi, 1965, 69).

Due to lack of reliable data there is no scientific representation of the numerical strength of the various religious groups in Nigeria and of their geographical distribution. Nevertheless, the Islamic faith exceeds in weight in the northwestern and northeastern parts of the country. On the other hand, Christianity is also more pronounced and well-known in the South-East and South-South geographical zones of Nigeria. The South-West and North-Central zones have a good balanced number of Muslims and Christians.

According to a 2001 report from The World Fact book by CIA, about 50 percent of Nigeria's population is Muslim, 40 percent are Christians and 10 percent adhere to local religions (Wikipedia, 2018). It was also observed from Pew Research that Nigeria has the world's fifth largest Muslims population and sixth Christians' population (Pew Research Center). In other words, there is significant number of Christians and Muslims in the country and this may be the main reason for the persistent violence between Muslims and Christians in Nigeria. There is another fighting going on at the time of writing this work among the Christians and Muslims in Ilorin over the wearing of *hijab* in a mission school which is getting out of hand presently as there were many people that have been brutally injured in the process.

THE THREE MAJOR RELIGIONS IN NIGERIA

Nigeria is a multi religious country for this reason it is not possible for a leader (Government or traditional rulers) to impose one religion over the people. The popular saying among the Yoruba that, *Oba ko lesin, gbogbo esin ni Oba nse* which means a paramount ruler (King) does not have a religion but participates in every religion of the land testifies to this reality. The three major religions in Nigeria are African Traditional Religion, Islam and Christianity. The African Traditional Religion (ATR) is the religion of the Aborigines. The practice of African traditional religion varies from one place to another that some people refer to it as religions; some are Ifa worshippers, some worship god of thunder and some, god of iron and some are Masquerade worshipers and the like. This work will discuss African Religions generally, though, ATR does not have a written scripture like Christianity and Islam but the adherents orally pass the faith from generations to generations through folk tales, proverbs, songs and festivals.

African Traditional Religion believes in the existence one supreme God who is the creator of the whole universe (both animate and inanimate) and the controller of human destiny (Otijele, 2). The Yoruba in Nigeria refer to Him as *Eleeda* (the creator) or *Olorun* (the owner of heaven) and as the owner of heaven, He controls both heaven and the earth. The Africans also believe that God, because of His majesty, cannot be approached directly if it is impossible for a person to go to the President of a country without consulting the aides of the President, how much more is the Supreme owner of the universe. Hence, there are other lesser gods (deities) such as *Ogun* (god of iron), *Sango* (god of thunder), and *Osun* (river goddess) *Eyo* (a Masquerade in Lagos) which serve as intermediaries of approaching the Supreme God. So, most Africans usually build shrines in their houses to worship and venerate these deities.

History reveals that the adherents of African Traditional Religion are tolerance and live peacefully with other faith groups. The *Ifa* oracle's prediction of Christian missionaries' arrival to Abeokuta corroborates this assertion in Omoyajowo's word as Dopamu quoted thus "As early as 1845 Ifa was said to have predicted the coming of the missionaries to Abeokuta, had declared favourably about the Christian practice and pleaded its missionaries be allowed to establish and practice their religion. When consulted on the arrival of the missionaries in the 1840s the oracle reaffirmed its earlier plea for tolerance" (Dopamu, 319, NY). So, Rotimi Omotoye stresses that the Yoruba traditional worshippers welcomed the Christian missionaries with open hands because the Ifa Oracle had earlier predicted the coming of the religion and at the same time, supported the settlement of Shehu who was a Muslim cleric from Ilorin in Abeokuta to propagate his faith (Omotoye, 2012, 334). This must have contributed to the warm reception of the Christian missionaries by King Sodeke (The Alake of Egbaland) and his subjects when they came for their missionary's activities. The adherents of ATR according to Ayandokun are devoted to their faith and this helps them to be committed to moral values (Ayandokun, 2019, 276) of which tolerance and harmonious livings are key.

Islam is a strict monotheistic religion, the followers believe in the worship of one God – Allah who has no beginning or end. Islam in Arab word means surrender or submission to the will of Almighty Allah; it has a written scripture called Qur'an which is considered verbatim words of Allah to his followers and it is infallible without error. The basis for Islam doctrine is found in the Qur'an comprises of 114 chapters arranged from the longest to the shortest. The five pillars of faith in Islam are

1. Shahadah means the confession of faith that Allah is the only one God
2. Salat means prayer and every Muslims prays five times a day
3. Sawn means Ramadan, it is the fast of the month of Ramadan compulsory for all Muslims
4. Zakat is alms-giving to the less fortunate
5. Hajj is the holy pilgrimage to Mecca at least once for every Muslim. ("Islam" @ https://en.wikipedia.org/wiki/Islam...)

Muslims also hold tenaciously to six articles of faith which are

a. Monotheism – the belief in one God who created the universe and He is the only one worthy of worship.
b. Belief in Angels as the messengers of God created to carry out God's instructions
c. Belief in the Prophets and Messengers, that God created humans and want us to live together in peace
d. Belief in the holy Books which are Torah, Bible and Qur'an
e. Belief in the day of Judgment
f. Belief in predestination ("Islam" @ https://en.wikipedia.org/wiki/Islam...)

The Muslims also emphasize that Islam is a religion of peace as the word Islam is derive from Arabic *salam* which means peace (Armstrong, 2001, Online). The acceptable way for a Muslim to greet a fellow Muslim is by saying *As-salam Aleykun* which means 'peace be unto you', the response to this greeting is *wa-aleykum salam* which means 'peace be also unto you'. Peace (*salam*) is also said to be one of the Ninety –nine beautiful names of God (Egbunu, 2012, 281). So Islam is not synonymous with terrorism.

Christian Religion is also monotheistic as the Bible says 'hear O Israel, the Lord our God, the Lord is one (Deuteronomy, 6: 4 NIV). It however emphasizes that God reveals himself as Father – the creator, Son – Christ the Redeemer and Holy Spirit – the Comforter. Thus, Christians belief in triune God, death and resurrection of Jesus Christ, Holy Bible, judgment and the like. Their name - Christian came from Christ who is the father of the faith. The Disciples of Christ were first called Christian in Antioch because they were behaving like their master - Christ (Acts 11:26). Christians were therefore expected to be like Christ who is a Comforter, Counselor Mighty God and the Prince of peace (Isaiah 7:7)

The moral values and the doctrines of all the three important religions practice in Nigeria are similar. All the religions preach against dishonesty, adultery, promiscuity, hatred and derive their teachings from their holy books, though ATR does not have a written scripture. Islam even belief in Torah and Bible while Christians similarly read Qur'an to get moral lessons. To this end, there are revelations of God in all the three religions, the adherents should therefore live together in peace and learn to accommodate one another. The main reason why people are affiliated to one religion according to Esther Ayandokun is because of their desire to be attached to a divine being and worship Him (Ayandokun, 2019, 278). Worshipping God does not call for fighting and killing as God Himself permits mankind to decide on what to do including whom to worship (Joshua 24:15). Arinze affirms that violence, terrorism, taking of human lives and destruction of properties are condemned by all genuine religions (Arinze, 2002, viii). He argues further that any genuine worship of God cannot but produce love and harmony in our relationship with fellow human beings and with the whole of creation. So, a true worshipper of God must eschew violent and embrace peace (Arinze, 2002, ix). Religious adherents should as a result learn to tolerate another for peace to reign in Nigeria.

CHAPTER TWO

RELIGIOUS VIOLENCE IN NIGERIA

This chapter discusses some identifiable causes of religious violence in Nigeria as well as x-raying some religious crises in the country with the aim of suggesting ways out of these crises.

Conflict is not entirely bad as there are some conflicts that have led to positive changes. On the other hand, conflict that results to violence and brutal killing must be avoided for it is capable of drawing a nation or organization backward. Violence today is a global crisis; it is not an issue peculiar to one country. There have been cases of violence in the Democratic Republic of Congo, the genocides in Rwanda between the Tutsis and the Hutus, ethnic and religious conflicts in Somalia, Ethiopia, Eritea, Angola, Nigeria, Liberia, Ivory Coast and the Sudan (Ogundipe, 2014, 220). European countries are not immune from this global phenomenon that has claimed lives of thousands of people.

The causes of violence are always complex. In the opinion of Akindehinde, violence is an attitude and an act rooted in personal and communal fragmentation. It is traceable to distorted, oppressive and unjust relations. It is often advanced by personal or collective human ideologies (Akindehinde, 2019, 1). Violence probably occurs among people because of the nature of man. God created human beings with the ability to make choices and the choice one person makes may not be the choice of another person which may eventually result into conflict. Violence in Nigeria as noted by Ojo ranges from Socio-political, ethnic, religion and domestic violence (Ojo, 2014, 208). In addition to the lists above Enyinnaya includes class differences as one of the plethora causes of Violence in Nigeria (Eyinnaya, 2008). Atowoju asserted that disagreement between Muslims fundamentalist and Christians is one of the reasons for incessant religious violence (Atowoju, 2008: 2). This is because most of the religious violence in Nigeria is between Muslims and Christians.

According to Jegede, among the causes of religious conflict in Nigeria are marginalization, oppression and government influence, uneven distribution of wealth and resources, division in government, nepotism and socio-religious bigotry. Religious conflict exists where there is disagreements between adherents of the one or different religion(s) over doctrinal issues or unjust treatments carried out against member(s) of a particular religion by members of the same or another religion due to incompatible religious interest or contradictory doctrinal issues (Jegede, 2019, 61)

Historical evidences in Nigeria have revealed that ethnic and perhaps religious violence has occurred ever since the inception of Nigeria as a Nation State. Bola Sebiowo in her argument to buttress this submitted that the first recognized religious violence in Nigeria took place in Southern Zaria in 1902 when Christian faith was introduced into Zaria Emirate by the Roman Catholic Mission which made the Muslim leaders resisted Christianity in the emirate and guide against its spread (Sebiomo, 2001, 69 – 72). Contrary to Sebiomo's submission Takaya traced origin of religious violence in the country to 1804 during Usman Dan Fodio Islamic political campaign. Dan Fodio's main intention for this was the religious purification of the north and establishment of Islamic state (Takaya, 1987, 17 – 19). Thus in Nigeria today, religion is either the root cause or has a link with prominent recorded violence, which is always between the adherents of the two major religions – Christian and Islam in the country. Some of the followers of these religions are claiming supremacy of one over the other. For example some Islamic fanatics believe that Islam is the only religion ordained by Allah, other religions are not from Him as some passages of Quran affirmed that 'surely the true religion with God is Islam' (Sebiomo, 2001: 71) So, efforts must be gear towards making every human being to become a Muslim. A statement credited to Shekau to the Christians corroborates this "The religion of Christianity you are practicing is not a religion of God it is paganism…We are trying to coerce you to embrace Islam, because that is what God instructed us to do" (Wikipedia, October 2018).

Christians on the other hand preach that it is only those who believe and accept Jesus Christ that will go to heaven as recorded in the holy Bible that "there is no other name under heaven given to men by which we must be saved (Acts 4: 12). Even Jesus Christ – the founder of the faith stated in John 14:6 that 'I am the Way, the Truth and the Life; no one comes to the Father except through me'. The claim of religious particularism has been the major bone of contention between the Christians and Muslims. The claims by some people that 'my religion is better than your own' or 'we are serving the true God' is nothing but religious bigotry which according to Alabi and Lateju is a major cause of religious violence in Nigeria. They stated that the lack of religious tolerance was revealed in the Newspaper report of January 10 concerning the religious riot in Jos which happened due to argument on encroachment of a church's land. The report states that "…some other said it (clash) began at a building site where a man, a Muslim, had encroached on the land belonging to a church. In the resultant argument, a fight had ensued" (Alabi & Lateju 2014: 126-127). In Jos city as well, there are some areas where Muslims fear to settle in case conflicts ensue between the Southern and Northern sections. Likewise in Kaduna state, southern area is predominantly dominated by the Christians while the Muslims dominated the Northern part. Whenever there is conflict, the predominant Christian south is haven for the Christians while the Muslims stay in the north.

Another cause of religious conflict between Christians and Muslims is the use of religious symbol as argues by Jegede. The use of *hijab* (total covering of head) by the Muslims women as a way of honouring the creator, Allah. The Muslims see nothing wrong in wearing *hijab* to school, even if the school was established by the Christians. This was the root cause of March, 2021 *hijab* crisis in Ilorin, Kwara state. The Government of the state has authorized the female Muslim students in the State to wear *hijab* in the public schools. This, the Christians vehemently opposed on the ground that

Christian mission schools were the heritage of the Christians and not for the Government, even the Muslims would not permit Christian activities in the Muslim schools control by the Government. The Christians staged a peaceful protest which the Muslims hijacked thereafter; the Christians and Muslims began to stone one another. This showed lack of tolerance between the two religion worshippers, slight argument between Christians and Muslims always leads to fight which may aggravate to killing and destruction of properties. Thousands of lives and properties have been lost to many of these crises in Nigeria. Various responses to religious violence especially the intervention of Government, interfaith religious dialogue, religious tolerance, harmonization of religious doctrines and the like have only helped to calm the tension but never solve the problem.

Religion as it is observed all over in the world especially in Nigeria influences human action and activities which include violent and non-violent activities. Religion basically ought to be a mean to foster peace and harmony but it is always a basis for riot in Africa (Adekola, 2019, 129). Most of the violence in Nigeria has religion connotation and this as discussed earlier have been happening even before Nigeria got independent. Alao Abiodun submitted that Nigeria has recorded more religious conflicts than the rest of Africa. (Alao, 2009, Online). It was also noted that most of these religious violence have occurred in the Muslim dominated northern part of Nigeria. Religion as a mean of worship a Supreme Being should never be a source of conflict; it should rather be a unifying factor because major world religions preach peace which is a central theme of all religions. This is noted in the submission of Akindehinde thus:

> Religion could ordinarily serve, and have a great potential to function as a tool for social harmony in many developing countries like Nigeria. But in reality, religion has functioned more as a motivation and encouragement for violence, thus its indication in some research works as a 'double-edged sword'. From time ancient, religious dogmatists have tried all they could to legitimise violence in the name of God. In recent times, acts of extreme violence in churches specifically such as terrorist attacks are often justified as 'holy warfare'. Over the years, religion has been the major cause of most violent conflicts around the world, and as such, being famous and gaining notoriety as one of the chief security challenges facing the world today. (Akindehinde, 2019)

An Overview of Religious Violence in Nigeria

Some people have argued that the incidence of religious violence has grown exponentially since the return to democratic rule in 1999. Contrary to this argument countless of religious crises have occurred before 1999. The notable one among them happened in 1957 few years to the country independent when the Christians in Northern Nigeria raised alarm that the Muslims are planning to compel everybody in the North to Islam. As a result of this according to Harry Boer, Christians cried out for 'fears of Islamitization pointing, to instances where they were either forced into Islam or were forced to undergo trials in Sharia courts'(Boer,2004, 60). Statistics on religious crises across the country however show that at least 95% of them occurred in the northern part of the country (Ezeanokwasa Jude 2009) while few are from the Southern parts of Nigeria.

Maitasine Sect

The Maitatsine riots were series of violent uprisings instigated by Islamist militants in northern Nigeria between 1980 and 1985 and represented northern Nigeria's first major wave of religiously-inspired violence. The riots prompted immense ethno-religious discord between Muslims and Christians. The Maitatsine's movement was led by Mohammed Marwa (died in 1980). He was popularly known by his nickname Maitatsine but also called Allah *Tatsine*). This man was a controversial preacher in Nigeria (*https://rlp.hds.harvard.edu/faq/maitatsine-riots*}.

Allah Tatsine came originally from *Marwa* in northern Cameroon. After his education he moved to Kano, Nigeria in about 1945, where he became known for his controversial preaching on the Qur'an. Maitatsine claimed to be a prophet, and saw himself as a *Mujaddid* in the image of Sheikh Usman dan Fodio. Although a Qoranic scholar, he seemingly rejected the hadith and the sunnah and regarded the reading of any other book but the Qur'an as paganism. Maitatsine spoke against the use of radios, watches, bicycles, cars and the possession of more money than necessary (*https://rlp.hds.harvard.edu/faq/maitatsine-riots*}

The British colonial authorities sent him into exile, but he returned to Kano shortly after independence. By 1972 he had a notable and increasingly militant follower known as *Yan Tatsine*. In 1975 he was again arrested by Nigerian police for slander and public abuse of political authorities· But in that period he began to receive acceptance from religious authorities, especially after making hajj, the Muslim pilgrimage to Mecca. As his followers increased in the 1970s, so did the number of confrontations between his adherents and the police. His preaching attracted largely a large numbers of youths, unemployed migrants, and those who felt that mainstream Muslim teachers were not doing enough for their communities. In 1979, Maitatsine rejected the prophet-hood of Mohammed and portrayed himself as an *annạbi* i.e. prophet By December 1980, Yan Tatsine continued his attack on other religious figures and the police, this forced the Nigerian army to become involved. The subsequent clashes with the army led to the deaths of about 5,000 people, including Maitatsine himself. Maitatsine died shortly after sustaining injuries in the clashes either from his wounds or from a heart attack {*https://rlp.hds.harvard.edu/faq/maitat sine-riots*}.

An article published by the *Sunday Trust Magazine* in 2010 states that the military cremated Maitatsine's remains, which now rest in a bottle kept at a police laboratory in Kano{ https://en.wikipedia.org/wiki/Maitatsine}. Despite Mohammed Marwa's death, Yan Tatsine riots continued into the early 1980s. In October 1982 riots erupted in

Bulumkuttu, near Maidaguri and in Kaduna to where many Yan Tatsine adherents had moved after 1980. Over 3,000 people died. Some survivors of these altercations moved to Yola, and in early 1984 more violent uprisings occurred in that city. In this round of rioting, Musa Makaniki, a close disciple of Maitatsine, emerged as a leader and Marwa's successor. Ultimately more than 1,000 people died in Yola and roughly half of the city's 60,000 inhabitants were left homeless. Makaniki fled to his hometown in Gombe, where more Yan Tatsine riots occurred in April 1985. After the deaths of several hundred people Makaniki retreated to Cameroon, where he remained until 2004 when he was arrested in Nigeria.

Maitatsine riots of 1980 did not only attack non-muslims because Muslims, Government officers lost their lives during the mayhem. Some analysts described Boko Haram terrorist group as an extension of the Maitatsine riots as many Muslims were attacked and properties belonging to Muslims were destroyed (https://en.wikipedia.org/wiki/Maitatsine).

Onuoha submits that the 1980 Maitatsine riots and the current Boko Haram sectarian violence are both product of rigid adherence to Sharia jurisprudence (Onuoha 2012). Boko Haram has claimed thousands of lives in Nigeria between 2009 till date while within 12 days, the Maitatsine uprising 1980 claimed 5,000 lives in the Northern part of the country. The Maitatsine uprising was believed to be the forerunner of religious insurgency in the Northern part of Nigeria {*https://www. naija.ng/1101391-Maitatsine-story-nigerias-bloody-religious-terror-80s-grandmothe r-boko-haram.html*}. As a result of the assertion above, Boko Haram insurgence in Nigeria would be discussed before highlighting other religious violence in the country.

Boko Haram Insurgence

The beginning of Boko Haram sect in Nigeria can be dated to 2002 founded by Muhammad Yusuf. It is formally identified by its members as *'Jama'at ahlis Sunnah lid Da'wa wal Jihad', which means* 'people committed to the propagation of the Prophet's teachings and Jihad'. The name of the sect - Boko Haram is loosely translated from the Hausa language translated as western education is sinful and probiting western culture. It was in 2009 that the country began to experience their disturbances and killings of innocent people in Borno State. The group began mass bombing, killings and destruction of properties after the killing of their leader – Muhammed Yusuf. and it is replica of Afghanistans, Taliban and the Al Qaeda. The major demand of this sect is the establishment of Islamic states and enthronement of Sharia law in all the Northern states no minding the fact that there are many non-Muslims residing in the areas. Boko Haram sect thus claimed responsibility for bombing churches, police stations, market places, banks, beer palours, in many northern states in Nigeria. The sect claims that it is fighting the enemies who have wronged its members through violence, arrest or economic neglect and corruption (Udo, 2012, 369)

Boko Haram attacks in Nigeria within three years, 2009 to 2012 was massive. According to Udo records the details of the attacks as follows:

a. Before 2009, Boko Haram attacked the people of Maiduguri, Borno State Capital and over 100 people were killed
b. July, 2009 the sect launch an uprising in the north east of Nigeria in which more than 800 people were killed in five days of fighting.
c. In 2011 about 550 people lost their lives in 115 separate attacks by the sect in Borno state.
d. November, 2011, Boko Haram attacked police headquarters, churches and Mosques in Damaturu, Yobe State and killed more than 90 people
e. December 25 2011 attacked carried out by succide bomber at St. Theresa Catholic church, Suleja on Christmas day which claimed scores of lives. More than 25 people were killed, 13 cars burnt and 9 apartments scattered by explosions at the frontage of the church. Three families were burnt to death in their vehicles after boarding to depart the church, 4 motor-cyclists were killed.
f. In February, 2012 a Catholic church was bombed in the city of Jos which claimed 2 lives and several others wounded
g. In 2012 also Boko Haram fighters bombed and attacked 9 churches in Damaturu, Yobe State where more than 90 people died
h. The bomb attack and gun battle in Kano on January, 2012 left 186 people dead.
i. On Thursday April 19, 2012 the sect bombed offices of major Nigerian Newspaper in Abuja and Kaduna killing 8 people. The sect claimed that it attacked *This Day* Newspaper to send a strong message to the media that it would no longer condone reports misrepresenting it in the press or blaming it for acts it knows nothing about.
j. On April 24, 2012 Boko Haram attacked Television viewing centre in Tundu Wada, Jos

Boko Haram has killed a lot of innocent people and wipes away the whole family in a day. Since the beginning of this insurgence, they have not sheath the sword till today

A summary of some others religious attacks in Nigeria are captured below:

1. In October 1982 there was clashes when Muslim believers in Kano were able to enforce their power in order to keep the Anglican House church from expanding its size and power base. They saw the church as a threat to the nearby Mosque, even though the Anglican House church had been there forty years before the building of the Mosque (https://en.m.wikipedia.org/wiki/Regious_violence)

2. In 1986, the militants' Muslim clash on Palm Sunday in Ilorin which disrupted Palm Sunday procession. Churches and Mosques were set ablaze and many people were injured in the mayhem. In May that same year, the Muslim community in Ibadan burnt down the Risen Christ Chapel at the University of Ibadan (Afella, 2012, 223)

3. March 6th-12th 1987 in Kaduna State (Kafanchan, Kaduna, Zaria) & Katsina in Katsina State - Muslim students attacked Christian students at College of Education in Kafanchan and Christians fought back. The fight later spread to other places and more than 150 churches were burnt and over 25 Christians killed.

4. March 1988 Kaduna Polytechnic, the Kaduna State Government destroyed a Christian Chapel under construction. This led to religious uprising.

5. 1988 - Kaduna State (ABU University Zaria) - Benson Omenka, final year student, killed by Muslim students during Students Union election. Christian students were also stoned, maimed and raped.

6. 1988 in Bauchi State, the religious conflict in Bauchi State Secondary Schools where Muslim students attacked Christian Teachers and students in GSS Gombe, GTC Gombe and GSS Bauchi and other Secondary Schools in Bauchi State. Thus, some of the Christian students were badly wounded.

7. April 20th-23rd 1991 in Bauchi State. Fighting between Muslims and Christians led to the death of more than 200 people and 700 churches and mosques were burnt.

8. October 14th-16th 1991 in Kano State. The Reinhard Bonnke riots fighting between Muslims and Christians as Muslim activists rampaged and protested against a planned revival meeting during which a German Evangelist, Reinhard Bonnke, was expected to be the guest preacher.

9. October 1991 in Plateau State. A young man from Anaguta was beaten to death on a field opposite University of Jos during election primaries of the defunct Social Democratic Party (SDP).

10. February 1992 Kano State Many Christians were massacred and churches destroyed.

11. February 1992 - Plateau State, Jos - A young Christian, married with one child, was beaten to death by Muslims as he was going home from an evening church meeting, at Yan Taya junction, Jos.

12. April 15th-16th 1992 in Kaduna state, Zangon Kataf local Government Area - What was supposed to be a communal riot between Christians and Muslims and spread throughout Kaduna State. Hundreds of people lost their lives and buildings were burnt.

13. May 18th 1992 in Zaria, Kaduna. Rev. Tacio Duniya of E.C.W.A, Rev. Musa Bakut and a host of others were murdered by Muslim fanatics.

14. April 12th 1994 in Jos Plateau State there was fighting between Muslims and Christians over the appointment of one Aminu Mato as chairman of the Caretaker Committee for Jos Local Government Area. 16 lives were lost and properties were destroyed.

15. 1999 in Borno State there was religious riots as the state government moved the idea of not allowing the teaching of Christian Religious Knowledge in Schools.

16. February 4th - 22nd 2000 in Kaduna State, Riots began after a Christian march opposing the implementation of Sharia law. Travelers were killed as they tried to escape from their vehicles. More than 1,000 people died in various clashes.

17. February & May 2000. Christians in Kaduna were attacked on two different occasions as Muslim fanatics protested against the delay in introduction of Sharia in the state.

18. May 16th 2000 in Kaduna state, Muslim youths destroyed ECWA in Kaduna only hours after peacekeeping troops left the area.

19. May 22nd 2000 in Kaduna state - Muslim youths torched the First Baptist Church and Christian homes, leading to retaliation by Christian youths. At least 11 people died and many others were injured in the incident.

20. May 25th 2000 - Kaduna state, several days of violence over the introduction of Sharia led to the death of at least 150 people. Homes, shops and churches were also destroyed.

21. September 7th-9th, 2000 Gombe State - In Bambam, 25 people died as a result of clashes between Muslims and Christians due to possible implementation of Sharia. Property damaged was estimated in millions of Naira.

20. June 2001 in Jigawa State, 15 churches and 14 Pastors and several residences were burned down in Gawaram. A similar attack on 11 churches occurred earlier in that year in Hadejia.

22. 5th August 2001 in Bauchi State According to the Church of Christ in Nigeria (COCIN), Muslim mercenaries had been attacking Christians in the Tafawa Balewa and Bogoro areas on two occasions. The attacks left more than 100 dead and 3,000 refugees.

23. 7th-12th September 2001 in Jos Plateau State, Muslims attacked Christians. Properties were destroyed and people lost their lives.

24. September 7th-17th 2001 - Kano State Seven churches were demolished; six churches set ablaze by a mob. Fifty four churches given demolition notices and seventeen churches demolished by the Kano state government. The Governor stated

that all churches in Shagari quarters of Kano city were "illegal structures", probably due to the religious conflict in Jos.

25. October 7th 2001. Muslim youths attacked three churches and 10 Christian-owned shops in Kaduna State with gas bombs, setting fire to the buildings.

26. October 14th-18th 2001 in Kano State as a result of Anti-American protests, 600 Christians were missing and another 350 were killed; at least five churches were burned during the resulting riots.

27. December 24th-25th 2001. A visit to Gombe State by the Israeli ambassador sparked a riot, at least 4 people were killed, 50 injured, and two churches damaged. 28. 2nd May 2002 - Plateau State, Jos_Muslims attacked Christians. Properties were destroyed and people lost their lives.

28. In 2002, an article wrote by the Nigerian journalist, Isioma Daniel on the Miss World Contest led to the demonstrations and violence that caused the death of over 200 people in Kaduna and *fatwa* (an Islamic death sentence) placed on her life. This made the 2002 Miss World contest moved from Abuja to London (Human Right Watch, Vol. 15, No.13, 23 July 2003)

29. May 2002 in Zamfara State, the whereabouts of two Christians charged with apostasy, converting from Islam to Christianity was unknown. Lawali Yakubu and Ali Jafaru disappeared after a judge refused to sentence them to death.

30. May-June 2002 - Niger State - At least 75 Christians were arrested for opposing the state's Sharia law

32. June 6th 2002 - Katsina State - A Christian Police Officer in Katsina was clubbed to death by a mob of Muslims after being accused of trampling a Koran. The Police Officer had warned a Muslim preacher to stop inciting violence against Christians. Afraid of being arrested, the preacher fabricated the Koran story to provoke the crowd.

33. September, 2002 in Kaduna State at Federal Government College Zaria, Muslim students fought against Christian students discovered that a Christian was likely to win the position of Students Union President during a student election. Many were killed and several female students raped.

34. October 13th 2002 - Kaduna, Zaria - A clash over a student election at the Federal College of Education in Zaria ended in the death of 20 Christian students.

35. November 20th-21st 2002 - Kaduna State, Kadoka and Kano, Muslim mobs ransacked *This Day* Newspaper's Office and then began to attack Christian targets, damaging up to 20 churches. Over 200 people were killed and 1,200 injured in the attacks.

36. December 26th, 2002 in Bauchi State. An armed Muslim mob attacked Christians concluding Christmas celebration. The Celestial Church of Christ and many Christian homes were burnt.

37. April 22nd 2003 in Kano State. A pastor and 6 of his members were killed in a house fire which was believed to have been set by Muslim militants.

38. December, 2003 in Plateau State, Rim Christians killed, houses and churches destroyed, individuals injured and many other damages.

39. February 2004 in Plateau State, Yelwa Shendam, 47 Christians burnt in church with a lot of houses and properties destroyed.

40. April 2004 in Kano State, Reprisal of Jos crises, many Christians were killed, houses and properties lost.

41. February 18th 2006 in Maiduguri, 56 churches burnt and 63 Christians killed in an orchestrated attack.

42. September 2006 in Jigawa State, 26 churches were burnt by the Muslim fanatics.

43. September 28th 2007 in Kano State, Tudun Wada 3 people were killed, 72 injured, 8 churches burnt.

44. December 2007 in Bauchi, Yelwa_Ten Christians killed and 47 injured.

45. May 13th 2008 in Bauchi State, Ningi, Tafawa Balewa Six churches burnt and vandalized.

46. November 28th 2008 in Plateau State over 100 Christians killed, 71 churches burnt, 1,647 families lost their homes, 535 businesses burnt.

47. December 2008 Sokoto NCCF (NYSC) bus burnt.

48. February 21st 2009 Bauchi 19 people dead, 12 churches burnt, 50 Christian houses destroyed.

48. 29th July 2009 Borno, Bauchi and Adamawa States A group called Boko Haram killed Christians who refused to accept Islam, burnt their churches and attacked security operatives.

49. 27th December 2009 in Plateau State. Muslims burnt Baptist Church at Yelwa and stabbed some Christians on the streets of Jos.

50. 29th December 2009 in Bauchi. A group called Kalikato attacked people in Bauchi, leaving 39 people dead and houses burnt.

51. 17th 21 January 2010_Plateau State_Muslims unleash destruction over 24 communities in Jos North, Jos South, Barkinladi, Mangu, Pankshin and Dangi, claiming numerous lives and burning Christian homes and Churches including Bukuru Market.

52. 20th January 2010 in Sokoto state. A Christian man was killed in retaliation over the incidence in Jos.

53. 22nd January 2010 in Kaduna State. Muslims attack Christians at Mararraban Rido (close to NNPC depot).

54. 28th January-1st February 2010 in Gombe State, Muslim fanatics burnt ECWA primary and secondary schools at Bolori, burnt houses belonging to Igbos at Duku, burnt Yoruba Hall at Jekadafari and also burnt two churches with one vandalized (*https://www.facebook.com/PrayForChristiansInTheNorthOfNigeria/post s/446091338845535* (assessed January 17, 2018)

CHAPTER THREE

EFFECTS OF RELIGIOUS VIOLENCE IN NIGERIA

Everything one does has consequences either positives or negatives and so is the religious violence in Nigeria. It is possible for one to conclude that there are only negative effects of religious crises considering the facts that many lives and properties are always lost during the menace. However, there are evidences that showed that not all conflicts are bad, so religious crises have made few positive impacts in the country and these are as follow:

1. Establishment of Interfaith Dialogues: - religious crises in Nigeria have resulted in establishing interfaith dialogues in the country. The first interfaith group, Advisory Council of Religious Affairs (ACRA) came to being during Gen. Ibrahim Babangida administration in 1986. This was due to disagreement between Christians and Muslims on permanent membership of Nigeria in Organization of Islamic Conference (OIC) where the country had been an observer since 1960. As a result of little or no impact in quenching the crisis, the Nigeria Inter-religious Council (NIREC) was founded when General Olusegun Obasanjo became the President and religious violence resurfaced.(Faseke 2012: 206). The essence of the interfaith conversation is not to show superiority of one religion over the other or to lay emphasis that one religion is savific which is usually the root of conflict. However, the essence is to discuss the common features that bring all the religions together especially in the Holy Bible and Holy Qur'an. One of these is the belief in Immaculate Conception of Jesus Christ which both Islam and Christianity affirmed.

   NIREC has therefore helped in putting end to some ethno-religious conflicts; one of it is the Bauchi crisis of December 11, 2007 when Muslims and Christians of Yelwa engaged in a deadly confrontation that started as a result of the erection of Mosque at Government Secondary School, Babantakko in the Yelwa area. The Mosque was said to have been destroyed twice by the Christians. After the second demotion, the group kept vigil to know the perpetrators. The Muslims staged a full scale assault on them and their supporters which lead several deaths and loss of properties. On the 31st of December, the co-chairmen of NIREC Alhaji Abubakar Sa'ad and Pastor Ayo Oritsejafor visited the area to sue for peace, and there was an immediate end to the problem as a result of NIREC intervention.

   Another good example of interfaith programme is The Abrahamic mission, a Nigerian Television Authority programme broadcasting nationwide every Friday 11:30pm to 12:30pm and repeated Sunday 5 -6 pm where an Islamic cleric and Christian cleric discuss together issues in Islam and Christianity capable of promoting peace and harmony. The telephone calls and messages from the viewers attested to the fact that, the programme has helped in dousing religious tension in Nigeria

2. Meeting the needs of aggrieved party: - Any time there is religious unrest, it means there are some injustices that the concerned people want to call the attention of the public to and to some extent some of these injustices have been meet. For example, in Kwara state during the administration of military Governor Jauji Kazir, Christians in the state showed their grievances over the appointment of members of ten government boards and parastatals that were all Muslims. The governor had to listen to the complaint of the Christians by appointing some Christians into the boards (Omotoye, 2012, 336). Similarly the 2002 Miss World Beauty pageants riot in Kaduna which came as result of a derogatory remark about Prophet Muhammad (SAW) in *This Day* Newspaper. The earlier displeasure of many Muslim organizations to the holding of the contest in Nigeria made the venue to be relocated from Nigeria to London.

There are however a number of adverse effects of religious riots in Nigeria. In the submission of Akindehinde, religious crises have severely affected social cohesion between Muslims and Christians and as well hindered the mutual trust. Thus, Muslims and Christians have become increasingly separate, withdrawing into their own communities in towns, suburbs and distinct rural areas (Akindehinde 2018: 3). The negative impacts of religious crises are further discussed below:

1. Destruction of Human lives: - One of the heinous effects of religious violence in Nigeria is the destruction of human lives. Many religious fanatics during clashes have in the name of being apologetic brutally and erratically killed people of opposite religion including women and children. They may even go to the extent of wiping out the whole family as *Scan News* reported that in Plateau State riot 'Gun men killed 10 members of one family'(Online). Sulaiman in his own argument submitted that different families have been affected in various ways during crises. Some have lost their bread-winners, children, and, at times, an entire family could have perished . Thereby due to religious uproar score of people have become orphans, childless, widow and widower. The record has it that, the 1980 Maitatsine disturbance in Kano left between 4,000 - 6,000 people dead (Olupona, 1992, 23 – 27). The April 1991 violence in Tafawa Balewa which occurred as a result of quarrel in the market between a Christian butcher and some Hausa/Fulani people. It was reported in this impasse that many Muslims and Christians were killed. Even the invitation of the army to restore order did not help the situation as a result of series of massacres in which thousands of people were alleged to have been killed' (Alanamu 2005: 165- 170; Armstrong 2014:10). Moreover, an estimated 3000 people were reported dead in a clash between Christians and Muslims in Kaduna

state in just only two days, February 20 and 21, 2000 (Olukorede, 2002, 8). Plateau state that was known as 'Home of Peace and Tourism' has also witnessed many religious riot resulting to massive killing of people. In 2001, between September 7 to 12 about 500 people lost their lives to religious violence and over 1000 people were seriously injured(Onyeka-Ben *et al.* 2004: 12). It is germane to state that, there is no religious riot in the country that did not claim lives or left many people badly injured. So many lives that could be useful for great transformation of the country have either been lost or made impotent due to religious violence mainly between Christians and Muslims.

2. Destruction of Properties: - Another adverse effect of religious riot is the destruction of private, public and religious properties by the fanatics. From the 1980 Maitatsine unrest till the present Boko Haram insurgence, Nigeria has witnessed diverse religious violence with heavy loss of materials and properties, many monuments of high and historical value have been destroyed. For example Shittu avowed that some rioters intentionally target social amenities provided for public convenience, which have nothing to do with their grievances. Street and traffic lights are vandalized at will, while government and private owned automobiles are set ablaze in some cases (Shittu 2013: 126-142). Similarly, properties and means of livelihood of some individuals suspected to be in rival religion are destroyed and this has dreadful effects on the nation's economy. Religious houses like churches and mosques are equally set ablaze which has end up in creating enmity, hatred and discord among the religious worshippers. The Nigerian Constitution stated that every citizen of this country has freedom of movement, association and to reside anywhere in the country. The religious affiliation has however hindered this to the extent there are some areas the Christians and Muslims cannot reside in their own country. Religion today is affecting the unity of Nigeria.
3. Creation of Camp for the displaced people: - The destruction of human lives during the unrest has as well led to the separation of many families who were running hectare scepter for their dear lives and has led to the creation of safety camp for the displaced people either by Government or Charity Organizations. Dogo in his submission affirmed that, *Boko Haram* insurgence has made over 3000 people displace (Dogo 2003: 33 – 37). Thousands of people have thus become homeless, displaced, and refugees in their own country depending on the support of Government and well meaning Nigeria to survive. This is also costing the government money that were not budgeted for which could have been spent on other pressing needs of the country to build refugee camp and provide other necessities like food, water, clothes for the affected people .
4. Negative image of the country abroad: - frequent religious unrest in Nigeria has affected the number of people who wish to come to Nigeria either for investment or tourist. Even many investors are relocating because they consider Nigeria as unsafe for any investment. For instance, Cadbury PLC

has relocated to Ghana likewise many textile companies which used to be source of income for many Nigerians are no longer operating in the country This has negatively affect the Nigerian economy and her development. In the word of Sulaiman:

> Religious violence tends to dent the image of the country in the international community. The frequent eruption of religious uprisings has forced some countries to issue travel warning advising their citizens not to travel to Nigeria because of religious tension that could erupt quickly and without warning. For instance, in December year 2003, the American State Department citing alleged resurgence of violence crises, warned its citizens of the dangers of traveling to Nigeria (Sulaiman 2016).

He submitted further that:

> In December year 2004, the Government of United States and Britain re-issued travel advice to their citizens traveling to Nigeria. The advisory noted among other things that ' religious tension between some Muslim and Christian communities results in occasional acts of isolated communal violence that could erupt quickly and without warning... '(Sulaiman 2016).

With the above information, so many investors and tourists do not want to come to Nigeria and even they come, they will stay for few days and return. The Nigerian citizen abroad are not helping the issue as many of they have seen their home country 'a no go' area for them.

5. Halting of Social Activities: - as Shittu rightly observed anytime there is outbreak of conflict in the country, social activities is usually affected. This is because Government do imposes dusk to dawn curfews in the affected areas in order to curtail further damage. This usually hinders the movement of people from engaging in their legitimate businesses and affects their daily income. Also, schools in the affected area could be shut by the authority and such would alter the school calendars. In the same way, the examinations in national and private educational institutions that coincide with communal disturbances are often subjected to postponement or cancellation. For example, due to insurgency, the 2013 Unified Tertiary Matriculation Examination (UTME) was not held in some Northern State of Nigeria. As a result of such prolonged unofficial holidays that are occasioned by religious and communal unrest, many students usually end up being school dropouts and constitute nuisance to the society (Shittu 2013: 126-142). Sulaimon also argued in line with the submission above that the incessant nature of violence in the country has negative impact of breeding social miscreant and criminals who by their access to weapons of war (which are usually sophisticated) become terrors to both their

immediate community and the larger society. The weapons are always difficult to retrieve after the crisis because most of these people are originally jobless and they often found solace in terrorizing the society (Sulaimon 2016). To this end, the future of Nigeria and the young ones who are the future leaders may be jeopardized if something is not done to curb religious violence.

The discussions above depict that there are more harms of religious violence than its gains. Therefore for peace and harmony to reign in the country, necessary steps must be taken to curb it. One of the key factors that can help in promoting peace and harmony in Nigeria will be the focus of the next chapter.

CHAPTER FOUR

THE ROLE OF RELIGIOUS LEADERS IN PROMOTING PEACE AND HARMONIOUS LIVING

The focus of this chapter is to discuss the role of religious leaders in ensuring peace and harmony in this country. The religious leaders in this context are those leading the three main religions in the country, such as Pastors, Reverends, Priests, Evangelists, Imams, Alfas and the like. Obaje listed some identities of religious leaders as, the people who believe that there is one God and this God is ultimately in control of the World which he created. The leaders who demonstrate commitments to religious truth and are eager to show the evidence of this truth in their daily conduct. The teachers of religion who demonstrate sound knowledge of what they believe and are eager to impart such to others, they have unquestionable commitment to teaching others what they believe and practice. They are promoters of the faith which has become part and parcel of them (Obaje 2001; 25 – 26)

Judging from what have been discussed above as the true likeness of the religious leaders. It is germane to say that these leaders have vital roles to play to curb the incessant religious unrest since they are respected and regarded as representative of God by the followers. Thus, the role they play will either promote or stop conflict. The writer will start quoting some utterances of religious leaders that are capable of igniting riot.

Some religious leaders are known for their provocating and hate speech with the use of loud speakers to attack their opponents while preaching or addressing their audiences. These have always been aiding and abetting their followers to engage in battle with their rivals. For example, Shabayang refers to the sermon recorded by The Middle East Media Research Institute (MEMRI) as *maledicta* i.e. religious hate and emphasized on what a particular preacher said in his message thus:

> Today we will talk about one of the distorted religions, about a faith that deviates from the path of righteousness... about Christianity, this false faith, and about the people whom Allah described in his book as deviating from the path of righteousness. We will examine their faith, and we will review their history, full of hate, abomination, and wars against Islam and the Muslims (Shabayang 2019: 247-248).

It was noted that, this same preacher debunked the dialogue of Muslims and Christians in finding solution to religious conflicts. He therefore attacked the doctrine of the Trinity and the centrality of the salvific redemption that was received through Christ in these harsh words:

> In this distorted and deformed religion, to which many of the inhabitants of the earth belong, we can see how the Christian deviate greatly from the path of righteousness by talking about the concept of the Trinity. As far as they are concerned, God is the Father, the Son, and the Holy Ghost: three who are one... They see Jesus, peace be upon him, as the son of Allah... It is the Christians who believe that Jesus was crucified. According to them, he was hanged on the cross with nails pounded through his hands, and he cried, 'My God, why have you forsaken me?' according to them, this was so that he would atone for the sins of mankind... Regardless of all these deviations, from path of righteousness, it is possible to see many Muslim... who know about Christianity only what the Christians claim about love, tolerance, devoting life to serving the needy, and other distorted slogans... After all this, we still find people who promote the idea of bringing our religion and theirs closer, as if the differences were minuscule and could be eliminated by arranging all those (interreligious) conferences, whose goal is political (Shabayang 2019: 248 - 249).

Abubakar Shekau, a Boko Haram leader was also quoted in one of his addresses to his audiences that:

> I want all Muslims in Nigeria and the world at large to know that this is a religious war between Muslims and Christians. Every Muslim should take note that this is not an ethnic war or any kind of war but a religious one. We have not started this work to finish in a week, month or year. The end of this war will be either they kill us or we emerge victorious. This war will not end until the very last one of us or Islam becomes the determinant of governance in Nigeria without question that will be the end of the war (Local News, Naij.com, October 2018)

The Christians are not left out in provocative utterances. The reaction of Catholic Archbishop of Lagos, Rev. Cardinal Olubunmi Okogie to the incessant killing of Christians in northern Nigeria is too harsh for a religious leader to say. He declared thus, 'we just want to keep Nigeria going just because of peace, but if anybody tries any nonsense this time, I don't care, I will burn the nation because it is going to be a religious war and nobody will dare stop anybody'(Ehioghae 2011: 363).

Also, the work of a popular Christian Author G. J. O. Moshay *Who is this Allah* (Moshay 2010) and *Anatomy of Qur'an* (Moshay, 2007) were done to present Islam negatively to the readers which could generate hatred between the two adherents. Similarly, a Protestant preacher Dr. Robert Morey founded a Crusaders Club which was organized into three tier-structure and sought for financial contributions to be made by members annually to promote the Christian faith. The statement of principle of all the three tier-structure depicts a hate speech as Shabayang quoted below:

> The religion of Islam stands to be the greatest threat against humanity that the world has ever known. I therefore agree with this statement and will pledge my support. I also understand that my donation will further the effort of Faith Defenders to reach these lost souls for the sake of Christ. I stand firm with Faith Defenders and further understand that at this time in history, we are in a crisis of epic proportion (Shabayang 2019: 251).

There is nothing bad when a person makes commitment to donate for expansion of a faith but for referring a religion as 'greatest threat against humanity' is capable of causing violence especially in Nigeria. This is not good for any religious leaders or followers to pronounce.

Another instance of utterance that could escalate violence was a statement credited to a respectable pastor and denomination leader which he said when he was preaching as follows: "I will not be the first to attack anyone, but if anyone attacks me, I will retaliate, there is no sin in defending yourself. Use Nehemiah approach to stop the incessant killing of the Christians'' (the Nehemiah approach he was referring to could be found in Nehemiah 4: 13 – 23 but the approach was not to kill anybody but to watch and prevent anyone from working to rebuild the broken wall of Jerusalem).

Some Christian leaders have been calling their followers to buy weapons and carry arms to protect themselves during religious violence. They justify their claim from Christ instruction to the disciples to sell their garment to buy sword in Luke 22: 36. But it was not sword alone that Christ told them to get, they are to look for purse, shoes and scrip. Actually what He was telling them was to make provision for the ministry and not to carry weapons. If He ordered the disciples to carry weapons why did He rebuke the disciple that used sword to cut one of His arresters' ears latter in Luke 22? (Adeloye 2018: 166). Origen as David Shenk quoted argued that as Christians "…no longer do we need to take the sword against any nation, nor do we learn war any more, since we have become sons of peace through Jesus Christ our author…" (Shenk, 2008, 7).

It is important to know that anyone who is saved by God will not encourage carrying of arms for religious violence (Audu, 2018, 27). The Christian message of love would be forfeited if they resort to killing the opponents that they want to convert. Killing will not even stop the opponents from attacking because it has never stopped it in the past; it will only continue to promote hatred, discord and bigotry. The message of Jesus Christ to His followers is to love, forgive and pray for those that persecute them (Matthew 5: 43).

One of the names given to Jesus Christ the founder of Christianity is the 'Prince of Peace' (Isaiah 9: 6). All the followers of Christ must be lover of peace and shun violence. Christ taught His disciples to always pray and forgive their enemies. An aspect of the Lord's Prayer reads 'forgive us our trespasses as we forgive those who trespass against us'. Man will definitely sin against God and offend fellow human being. It is human to sin because man has inherited sin from Adam but it takes a man with the heart of God to forgive. Christ did not only preach forgiveness, He showed a living example to His disciples. Luke 22: 47 – 51 reveals a non-violent spirit of Christ when a disciple cut the right ear of one of the High priest's servants that came to arrest their Master. He rebuffed the disciple thus "no more this..." this means no more violence. Christ later healed the affected servant to show retaliation is not the best option to religious violence (Adeloye 2018: 165 -166).

Religious leaders are to be promoter of peace and not to encourage retaliation during crisis because the creator God initiated peace to ensure everything goes well. The presentation of Pope Benedict XVI during 2013 world peace day corroborates the assertion that God is the initiator of peace, he said "Peace is an aspect of God's activity, made manifest both in the creation of an orderly and harmonious universe and also in the redemption of humanity from sin" (Benedict, 2013). Adeloye argues that the desire of God for peace and to rescue man from eternal damnation made Him to send Jesus Christ to reconcile the fallen world to Him. God loves peace and wants the whole world to be at peace and this made Him to initiate peace (Adeloye 2018: 165). So if God who the Muslims call Allah, who is Yahweh in Judeo-Christianity is the initiator of peace then the people that worship Him must be lover of peace. The religious leaders who the people see as man of God or servant of God must promote peace through their utterances in public and when preaching

Adeloye presented that Christian leaders are to perform the roles discussed below in promoting peace and harmony. It is however not limited to Christian leaders but all religious leaders.

1. Interceding for the Country: - Violence in Nigeria and any other country cannot be solved by man but by God who is the originator of the world and the only one that can provide lasting solution to human problem. Christian leaders as God's representative can mediate during violence not minding whether or not Christians are being attack by organizing persistent prayer for peaceful resolution of the problem at hand. A continuous prayer organize by righteous people to seek the face of God will help in ending the problem. This is in line with what God said "if my people which are called by my name, shall humble themselves, and pray, and seek my face, and turn from their wicked ways; then will I hear from heaven, and forgive their sin, and will heal their land" (2Chronicles 7: 14). God loves peace but the wickedness of man is the root cause of violence and other evils. If man can therefore deals with the sinful nature and return to God in prayer, peace would return to the land. Nathan Soderblom argued that peace can only be reached only through fighting the ancient Adam in ourselves and in others" (Soderblom, 1930). The ancient Adam in man can be destroyed with the power of prayer and peace will return to the land. Joint prayers can also be organized by the religious leaders this is to substantiate Fatokun's submission that Christians and Muslims could gather

for joint prayers not minding their religious differences to cry to God in prayer to save Nigeria (Fatokun, 2013, 318). This would promote peace if it is done regularly.

2. Emphasis on message of love: - the main teaching of Jesus Christ to his followers focused on love. He said in one of his teachings to His disciples that "You have heard that it was said, 'Love your neighbor and hate your enemy'. But I tell you: Love your enemies and pray for those who persecute you, that you may be sons of your father in heaven" (Matthew 5: 43 – 46). Jesus Christ during His earthly ministry was persecuted several times by the Jews. He was arrested, beaten, molested and crucified but He did not repay His persecutors with evil instead He prayed for them 'father forgive them for they don't know what they are doing' to justify His teaching. Apostle Stephen similarly prayed that God should not hold the sin against those that stoned him. This was done out of genuine love he has for the people, he knew his persecutors were not save and they need to be saved. Church leaders should therefore intensify more effort in mission and evangelism and show love for non-Christians by assisting, praying and care for them. Apostle Paul buttresses this by saying "If your enemy is hungry, feed him; if he is thirsty, give him something to drink…" (Romans 6: 20). Through this, some of them will be won and there would be peace in the land.
3. Preaching message of forgiveness:- Christ in His teaching also enjoined His followers to forgive their offenders. Christ similarly taught them to forgive so that the heavenly father would forgive them. The Christian that fails to forgive would not be forgiven. Christian leaders should use the privilege of leading Christian community to always preach forgiveness and never to encourage the followers to fight back. If a Christian fights back and die along with the non-Christians. Such Christian would not only go to hell but would be condemned for murder and failure to rescue the unbelievers (Ezekiel 33: 8). As a Christian just as Martin Luther King Jr. insisted and quoted by Onuche thus:

> We must develop and maintain the capacity to forgive. He who is devoid of the power to forgive is devoid of the power to love. It is also necessary to realize that the forgiving act must always be initiated by the person who has been wronged, the victim of some great hurt, the recipient, of the same torture, injustice, the absorber of some terrible act of oppression (Onuche, 2018, 81 – 82).

Christian must therefore cultivate the habit of forgiving the offenders because that is what the Master expects from all believers.

4. Preaching reconciliatory messages:- The whole world has sinned against God as a result of sin inherited from Adam and Eve but reconciled through the atoning work of Jesus Christ. The Bible says God has reconciled us to himself by Jesus Christ and has given to us the ministry of reconciliation (2Corithians 5: 18). The message of reconciliation has been given to Christians by Christ. It is mandated of all religious leaders to proclaim message that will lead to reconciliation

anytime there is riot, their action and attitude must promote peace. As respected religious leaders they must avoid unguarded word that could make their naïve followers to look for arms and weapons to fight whenever there is violence as such action will aggravate the problem. If fighting is the option and Christians succeeded in killing all the enemies of the faith, then who would be the target of the Christians again? So, Christian messages should be the one that will heal the wound in order to gain converts to Christian faith. A great lesson could be learnt from the early church that were not move by the persecution but still scattered abroad preaching messages of reconciliation (Acts 8: 4 - 13). This made the church to have more converts and this support Tertullian's assertion that "the blood of the martyrs is the seed of the gospel". In addition, in his own submission, Obaje declared that religious leaders must promote a nation of reconcile ethnic groups in their daily preaching and admonition they are responsible to unite all ethnic groups to see one another as real blood brothers and sisters, created in the same image of one true God (Obaje 2001:30). Christians and Muslims traced their origin to Abraham, the father of Isaac and Ishmael. So the two religious adherents must see themselves as descendants of Abraham that must dwell peacefully together without resentment.

5. Educating the people on Christian's doctrine: - many Christians don't know the tenets of their faith and never bother to know since they are not pastors. It is the responsibility of the Christian leaders to educate their followers to know the doctrine or tenets of Christian faith. The early apostles did well in educating their converts during the formative years of the church and the converts were devoted steadfastly to the apostles' doctrine (Acts 2: 42). If they were not taught how would they be devoted to the doctrines of the apostles? Most Christian leaders don't have time for Bible teaching which is necessary for their members to know the mind of God. Apostle Paul said in his Epistle to Ephesus that the gift of teaching is one of the gifts that Christ gave to the church and this must be used to perfect the Saints (Ephesians 4: 11-12). Christian leaders must continue to educate their followers to grow in the knowledge of God for them to shun violence and all evil desires. So, the education that would be given to them must be well prepared, relevant, transforming, flexible, varied and designed to change behavior of the receivers (Malcor, 2001, 45) and make them to be useful for God.
6. Be a living example: - Christian leaders should also live by what they teach for them to change behavior of their audience. They must not only preach love and forgiveness they must also show genuine love to every inhabitant of the land irrespective of religious affiliation. They must be actively involved in settlement of dispute through mediation and arbitration (Soderblom, 1930). Christ was actively involved in settlement of dispute during his earthly ministry. He intervened when the woman caught in adultery was brought to Him to be stoned as it was in the Law of Moses. The response of Jesus made all the accusers to leave her. Thus the spoken word of Christian leaders during riot may help to put an end to religious crisis (Adeloye 2018: 166 – 169).

7. According to Obaje, religious leaders have the responsibility of building a nation of God-Fearers. This could done through the messages and counsel they give to their followers and it will help to promote faith in one God and prompt spiritual awakening to hate all evils including shedding of blood.
8. Build a nation of patriotic and responsible citizens where every inhabitant will be loyal to God, loyal the country, safeguard human lives and properties and strive to defend the unity of the country
9. Inspire a nation of love and peace where every citizen shall experience true love and peace shall touch every heart and everywhere shall be saved for every religious adherent to live.
10. Inspire a nation of truly religious people that serve the Lord with their whole heart and obedience to God's injunction (Obaje 2001: 29 – 32).

CHAPTER FIVE

CONCLUSION AND RECOMMENDATIONS

Nigeria had witnessed many religious conflicts especially from 1980 till date. Some of the causes and effects of these conflicts were discussed in this work. It was noted that the major cause of religious violence is the inability to tolerate the religious teachings. The Holy Books of the two major religions in Nigeria enjoin the practitioners to practice their faith without compulsion. The Holy Qur'an affirms that religious worship should be left for the individual, since the right path is distinct from the wrong path and everyone is free to decide on which path to take.. Surah 2: 256 - 257 records that;

> There is no compulsion in religion. Verily, the right path has become distinct from the wrong path. Whoever disbelieves in *Taghut* (false leaders and false deities) and believes in Allah, then, he has grasped the most trustworthy handhold that will never break. And Allah is All-Hearer, All-Knower. Allah is the *Wali* (Protector or Guardian) of those who believe. He brings them out from darkness into light. But as for those who disbelieve, their *Auliya* (Supporters and Helpers) are *Taghut* (false leaders and false deities), they bring them out from light into darkness. Those are the dwellers of Fire, and they will abide therein forever.

Similarly, the Holy Bible states: For it is written, as I live, saith the Lord, every knee shall bow to me, and every tongue shall confess to God. So then everyone...shall give account of himself to God. Let us not therefore judge one another anymore...(Romans 14: 11 -13). The quotations from the Holy Qur'an and Holy Bible above show that each individual is responsible for his/her action no one should be coerce to practice religion against his/her wish. No religious practitioner should call people in rival religion infidel, so the agitation by some religious fanatics to fight until everybody in the world practice one religion is against the teaching of the two sacred scripture. Religious leaders should inculcate into their adherents mutual respect for human lives and their religions. Religious tolerance is the key for peaceful co-existence. It is germane to say that, religious tolerance is not against spreading one religious belief but it is totally against coercing people to accept one's faith or claiming a religion to be the true faith while others are inferious and not serving the real God.

As submitted in this work majority of the religious conflicts were as a result of the provocative utterances of religious leaders especially during religious mayhem. The author argued that religious leaders are respected by their followers; they are therefore in the best position to call the followers to order, teach them the right doctrine of the Holy Books to love others with the love of God, allow peace to reign and follow the path of peace of all the three religions in Nigeria. Christians are serving Jesus Christ 'the Prince of Peace' who says 'Peace I leave with you; my peace I give you, I do not give you as the World gives...(John 14:27 NIV). The Muslims are the followers of Prophet Muhammad (SAW) and the Prophet himself gave support to Christians during his time. The Holy Qur'an is believed to have come down on the Night of power and peace (Qur'an 97:5).Islam is religion of peace that encourages its adherents to strive for the enthronement of goodness and repulsion of evil in every circumstance and accommodate plurality of creed, ideologies and philosophies (Egbunu2012:282). The Africa Traditional Religions though do not have a written scripture but its moral practices are pass orally from one generation to another. Africans have values for human lives which is seen in their religions. For Example one Odu *Ifa* says in Yoruba *ema si ka laye nitori e o rorun, nitori be 'de bo'de e o ro'jo*. (This means do not engage in evil because you will leave this world or go to heaven, when you get to the boundary of heaven and earth you will give account). There is nothing done under heaven that is not recorded whether good or bad. So, all religious adherences should wage war against all evil practices including killings and destruction of properties and give peace a chance. Conclusively, according to Ismail and Kannike:

> Peace and peaceful co-existence in Nigeria or any other nation or society depend on perfect adherence to the tenets of the religions i.e. the Qur'an and Sunnah the Prophet (SAW), for the Muslims and the Holy Bible for the Christians. Piety is not only the beginning of wisdom, or the only path to success in life but also the only way to attain salvation which is the essence of life... (Ismail and Kannike 2018: 120)

The religious leaders are the only one that can explain the tenets of their religions and to lead them to eternal salvation. When this done, peace and harmony will reign in the country. The religious leaders thus have tremendous roles to perform to ensure peaceful co-existence in Nigeria.

RECOMMENDATIONS

Base on all the arguments presented in this work, the following recommendations are made to promote peace and harmony in Nigeria

1. The Religious leaders must avoid uttering provocative words during or before crisis no matter the circumstances and should always teach their followers to eschew violence and serve as agent of peace
2. The religious leaders must devote more times to teaching the doctrine of their faith to the followers as well as read and explain their Holy Books to guide against wrong teachings.
3. The religious leaders must follow the peaceful co-existence of their religious founder. Jesus Christ preaches love and harmonious living, Prophet Muhammad (SAW) enjoins Muslims not to argue with people of Scripture (Jews and Christians) Qur'an 29:46. The Prophet also signed treaty with Christians of Sinai Land and request his followers to kind to them and respect them (Ayinla 2018: 104)
4. All religious adherents must be tolerance and ready to accommodate one another despite different ways of worshipping God
5. More efforts should be intensified on interfaith dialogue to know what other faith adherences believe, talk and deal with possible causes of conflict and have respect for all religious founders.
6. The Government as well should not favour or support one religion over the others since Nigeria is a multi religious society. No religion should be declare a state religion either by the State Government or Federal Government

REFERENCES

Abogunrin, S. Oyin 2001, 'Religion and National Rebirth: The Nigerian Experience' in *Orita Ibadan Journal of Religious Studies*, xxxiii, Vol. 1-2, June and December

Adekola, O. Oluwawunsi 2019, 'Religious Studies Education for Peace and Sustainable Development in Nigeria', in Akubor Emmanuel Osewe and Shabayang Barnabas Sama'ila (eds.) *Religious Education and Nation Building: Nigeria and the world in the 21st century* (Ibadan, Darosat Global limited,

Adeloye, Gabriel Oludele 2018, 'The Roles of Christian Leaders in Promoting Peaceful Coexistence in Nigeria, in Oyeneye, I. O et'al eds. *Religion, Education and Peaceful Co-existence: A Publication National Association for the Study of Religions and Education (NASRED)*

Afella, Terna 2012, "Religious Morality: Panacea or Bane for Nigeria? In Alana, Emmanuel O. (eds.) *Religions: Journal of the Nigerian Association for the Study of Religions*, Vol. 22. No. 2, July, 2012.

Akindehinde, Adewunmi 2018, "The Impact of Persistent Violence on Church Growth and Development in Northern Nigeria" B.Th Long Essay Submitted to the Faculty of Baptist College of Theology, Lagos.

Alao, Abiodun 2009, 'Islamic Radicalisation and Violence in Nigeria' http//www.securityanddevelopment.org/pdf/ESRC%20Nigeria%20Overview.pdf. accessed 22nd February, 2021.

Alanamu, A.S. 2005, Reflections on Religious Violence in Nigeria (19992004). In Alanamu, A.S. (eds.): *Issues in Political Violence in Nigeria.* Ilorin: Hamson Printing Communication.

Ajayi, J. F. Ade 1965, *Christian mission in Nigeria1841 – 1891: The making of A New Elites*, London, Longman Group Ltd

Arinze, F. 2002, Religions for Peace – A call for Solidarity to the Religions of the World, New York, Longman and Todd

Audu, Samson Iliya 2018, "the Church's Participation in Mission as a Response to Religious Violence in Nigeria" in B*TSK Insight,* Vol. 15, No. 2

Ayandele, E. A 1966, *The Missionary Impact on Modern Nigeria 1842 – 1914: A Political and Social Analysis,* Britain, Longmans

Ayandokun, Esther O 2019, 'The Role of Religious Leaders in Creating An Atmosphere for Peaceful Co-existence among Faith Groups in Nigeria', in Akubor Emmanuel Osewe and Shabayang Barnabas Sama'ila (eds.) *Religious*

Education and Nation Building: Nigeria and the world in the 21st century Ibadan, Darosat Global limited.

Ayinla, Olawuwo Abdul Fatai 2018, 'Islamic Principles to Achieving Peaceful Religious Co-Existence in Our Contemporary Society', in Oyeneye, I. O et'al eds. *Religion, Education and Peaceful Co-existence: A Publication National Association for the Study of Religions and Education (NASRED)*

Atowoju, A. A. 2008, 'Exemplifying the Parable of the Good Samaritan (Luke 10:37) for a Peaceful Christian-Muslim co-existence in Nigeria' A paper presented in *West African Association of Theological Institution* (*WAATI) Conference*

Benedict Francis XVI 2013, "Blessed are the Peacemakers" being a presentation at the 2013 World Peace Day

Boer, Harry 2004, "Christians: Why We Reject Muslim Law" *Studies in Christians-Muslims Relations*, Vol. 7.

Dopamu, Abiola P NY, "Religious Pluralism in Nigeria: The Example of the Yoruba" in Ade P. Dopamu et al, eds. *Dialogue Issues*

Egbunu, Fidelis Eleojo 2012, "Religious Pluralism and the Quest for Peace in Nigeria" In Alana, Emmanuel O. (eds.) *Religions: Journal of the Nigerian Association for the Study of Religions*, Vol. 22. No. 2.

Ehioghae, E.M. 2011. 'Religion and Violence in Contemporary Nigerian Society: A Proposal for Peaceful Co-Existence', in Akanmidu, R. A. ed. *Thoughts in the Humanity*, Ilorin: Decency Printers & Stationary Ltd

Eyinnaya, John 2008, "Terrorism, Jihad and Just War: A Study of Christian and Islamic Approaches to Religious and Political Conflicts in Nigeria" A Paper presented at the *West African Association of Theological Institution (WAATI) Conference.*

Fatokun, S. Adetunji 2013, "Christian-Muslims Relations in Nigeria: Cooperations and Conflicts" in *Christianity and African Society*, Ibadan, Book Wright Publishers Nigeria Limited.

Faseke, Babajinmi O 2019 "Forging An Interfaith Cooperation in A Multi-Religious Society: The Case of Nigeria Inter-Religious Council (NIREC), 1999-2015", in Akubor Emmanuel Osewe and Shabayang Barnabas Sama'ila (eds.) *Religious Education and Nation Building: Nigeria and the world in the 21st century* Ibadan, Darosat Global limited.

Ismail, Muhammad Hadi and Kannike, Hassan Muhammad 2018, 'Islaic Concept of Peace and Peaceful Co-Existence in Nigeria Milieu', in Oyeneye, I. O et'al eds.

Religion, Education and Peaceful Co-existence: A Publication National Association for the Study of Religions and Education (NASRED)

Malcor, R. Carvin 2001, 'Christian Education in the Local Church', in *New Horizons,* April 2001.

Obaje, Yusuf Amen 2001, "The Role of Religious Leaders in National Rebirth" in *Orita Ibadan Journal of Religious Studies*, xxxiii, Vol. 1-2, June and December

Ogundipe, S. O 2014, "Conflict and Violence in Nigeria: A Christian Ethics Concern", *Practical Theology: Journal of Baptist College of Theology, Lagos,* No. 7

Ojo, E. A. 2014, "Promoting Peaceful Co-existence in Contemporary Nigeria", *Practical Theology: Journal of Baptist College of Theology, Lagos,* No. 7

Omotoye Rotimi 2012, Religious Crises and their Management in Yorubaland: A Panacea for Nigerian Security and Development, In Alana, Emmanuel O. (eds.) *Religions: Journal of the Nigerian Association for the Study of Religions*, Vol. 22. No. 2

Olupona, J.K 1992, *Religion and Peace in Multi-faith Nigeria.* Ile-Ife: Obafemi Awolowo University.

Onuoha, Freedom C. 2012, The audacity of the Boko Haram: Background, analysis and emerging trend. *Security Journal,* 25, 135 – 151

Otijele, P. Yakubu 1991, "Understanding the African Worldview: A Religious perspective," In *Ogbomoso Journal of Theology*, No. 6

Osaghae Eghosa E. and Rotimi T. Suberu 2005, A History of Identities, violence, and stability. In Nigeria Centre for Research on Inequality, Human Security and Ethnicity, No. 6

Sebiomo, Bola 2001, 'Religious Violence in Nigeria: The Causes, Effects and Panacea for Minimizing it', in *Religious Forum Academia,* Vol 1, Ijebu-Ode

Shabayang, Barnabas Sama'ila 2019, 'Fundamentalism in Multi-Religious Society', in Akubor Emmanuel Osewe and Shabayang Barnabas Sama'ila (eds.) *Religious Education and Nation Building: Nigeria and the world in the 21st century* Ibadan, Darosat Global limited

Shenk, W. David 2008, "three Journeys: Jesus-Constantine-Mohammad" in *Mission in Context of Violence* Keit E. E.tel ed. Pasadena, William Carrey Library

Shittu, Abdulazeez Balogun 2013, 'An Overview of the Consequences of Ethno-Religious Violence in Nigeria: Implications for Muslim-Christian Relations ', in *Al-Asaalah International Journal*, vol. 4, no, 1, pp. 126-142

Sulaiman, Kamal-deen Olawale 2016, 'Religious Violence in Contemporary Nigeria: Implications and Option for Peace and Stability Order' in *Journal for the Study of Religion,* Vol. 29, No. 1, Pretoria

Soderblom, Nathan 1930, "The Role of Church in Promoting Peace" being 1930 Nobel Lecture" www.nobelprize.org, accessed 12th November, 2018

Takaya, B. J. 1987, "Ethnic and Religious Roots of Kaduna Mafia," in *The Kaduna Mafia: A Study of the Rise, Development and Consolidation of a Nigerian Power Elite* B. J. Takaya and S. G. Tyoden eds. Jos, University Press

Udo, Essien Manasseh 2012, "The Implication of Religious Terrorism for National Security," In Alana, Emmanuel O. (eds.) *Religions: Journal of the Nigerian Association for the Study of Religions*, Vol. 22. No. 2.

Maitasine Riots – Religious literacy project – Harvard University *https://rlp.hds.harvard.edu/faq/maitatsine-riots* (assessed January 17, 2018)

Maitasine@https://en.wikipedia.org/wiki/Maitatsine (Accessed January 2018)

"Maitasine – Story of Nigeria's bloody religious terror of the 80s" *https://www.naija.ng/1101391-Maitatsine-story-nigerias-bloody-religious-terror-80s-grandmother-boko-haram.html* (assessed January 17, 2018).

www.accord.org.za Ethnic and religious crises in Nigeria

'Pray for Chrisitians in Northern Nigeria' (*https://www.facebook.com/PrayForChristiansInTheNorthOfNigeria/posts/446091338845535* (assessed January 17, 2018)

http://scannewsnigeria.com/news/gunmen-kill-10-members-of-one-family-in-plateau-state/ (accessed, 17 May, 2021).

www.ingramcontent.com/pod-product-compliance
Lightning Source LLC
LaVergne TN
LVHW020313110826
845148LV00017BA/2651

* 9 7 8 1 6 3 9 0 2 5 6 3 3 *